# cup

a vibrant vessel of learning and creativity

*by Bridgette Towle and Angela Heape | edited by Ann Pelo and Margie Carter*

ISBN 978-0-942702-14-9

Printed in Korea by Four Colour Print Group, Louisville, Kentucky.

Kids' Domain Early Learning Centre
kidsdomain.co.nz
kidsdomain@adhb.govt.nz

The photos appearing on page 34 are used by permission of
Auckland Art Gallery.

Typeset in Agency FB, A Little Sunshine, Calibri and Century Gothic.

For more information about other Exchange Press publications and
resources for directors and teachers, contact:

Exchange Press
7700 "A" Street
Lincoln, NE 68510
(800) 221-2864 • ExchangePress.com

## A Call to Reimagine Our Work

The stories in the *Reimagining Our Work* (ROW) collection are anchored in the conviction that another world is possible for early childhood education—a world characterized by open-hearted and attentive collaborations between children and educators, in shared exploration of engaging ideas. This collection helps us begin to imagine that world, as we reimagine our work, moving beyond the joyless land of prescribed curricula with its corresponding outcomes and assessments, into the unpredictable, green-growing terrain of lively curiosity and rigorous critical thought.

Too often in our field, the discourse about educators reflects a diminished and disrespectful view of their capabilities for challenging, rigorous, generative thought. "Keep things simple and easily digestible," is a common caution. "Teachers want strategies that they can put immediately to use in their classrooms. Don't offer too much theory, too much complexity."

We disagree. **Strongly.** We believe that educators hunger for deeper meaning in their work. We believe that educators long to be challenged into their biggest, deepest, most startling thinking and questioning. We believe that educators are ready to have their hearts cracked open and their imaginations ignited. We believe that educators are eager to explore how theory looks in everyday practice and how practice can inform theory. These convictions are at the heart of this collection of stories.

In these stories, children and educators take up ideas of substance, pursuing questions in ways that are unscripted and original. They braid fluid imagination and expansive awareness into their collaborative inquiry. The children in these stories aren't "gifted" or privileged—except by the gift and privilege of their educators' potent regard for their capability, and their concomitant willingness to bring their best minds and hearts to the table.

Which is just what we see the educators do in these stories.

We hear educators reflect—in their unique voices and contexts—on their evolving understandings of children's capacities, and their roles as educators, and the meaning and practice of teaching and learning. The educators in these stories hold assumptions and visions different from the dominant paradigm in our field, and we have much to learn from them.

With the ROW collection, we hope to advance the conversation among early childhood educators, administrators, community college and university educators, policy makers and funders about the nature and practice of early education—a conversation which we also engage in the foundational book for this collection, *From Teaching to Thinking: A Pedagogy for Reimagining Our Work*. As you read, we hope that you are challenged, exhilarated, unsettled, and rejuvenated. We hope that you find kinship in these stories. We hope that the stories in this collection carry your thinking far beyond curriculum ideas, and help you reimagine your work. May these stories sustain you as you stand strong with the children in your care. Resist the limitations of standardized curriculum, and claim, instead, the exhilaration of creating a new world, together with children.

—*Ann Pelo* and *Margie Carter*
  Editors of the *Reimagining Our Work* (ROW) Collection
  Authors of *From Teaching to Thinking: A Pedagogy for Reimagining Our Work*

For more information on the ROW collection and upcoming titles please visit ExchangePress.com/ROW

## Cup

*The important thing about a cup*

*is that you can build with it.*

*It is round.*

*It stands up and you can balance it*

*on your head.*

*It shines really light in the dark,*

*and makes a loud noise*

*when it falls.*

*If you squeeze it, it will crack*

*and open up.*

*But the most important thing about a cup*

*is that you can build with it.*

A poem by Daniel C, Isobel S, Tia, and Harry

# assemble

# foreword

A bumble bee lands on a flower and unhooks her flight muscles from her wings so that she can vibrate her wings without taking off. The wings' vibration is music—an audible middle C—and that sweet music inspires the flower to release its pollen. It's a small act of magic.

A stack of cups beckons from the shelf. The cups' delicate translucence, their concave sturdiness, their quiet demeanor call to the children, and a relationship begins: cups invite and provoke and seduce the children and the children transform and animate the cups. It's a small act of magic.

Who leads the dance of bees and pollen, of cups and children? What begets what?

In their enthralling book, Bridgette Towle and Angela Heape explore the dynamic interplay of cups and children, inviting us to look at objects—and at children—in new ways.

As they tell the story of an unexpected, year-long immersion in cups, these two masterful teacher researchers illuminate the full-hearted, deeply thoughtful work of education. We listen as they consider what compels the children about the cups, and how they might join the children's dance with cups as active participants inquiring alongside the children and the cups. Because they ponder, confer, and experiment, the decisions that Bridgette and Angela make as educators are intentional; they trust each other and their intuition, they challenge each other and their understandings. With the steady support of their director, they consistently risk the unknown. When educators work in this way, they are sure to meet new discoveries, but who could have predicted that exchanges between children and cups would bring about such a vital intellectual journey?

Angela and Bridgette frame the story of cups with verbs that spark: *construct, transform, collaborate, imagine, theorise, connect, listen, provoke, embody.* These strong words describe not only the children's engagement with cups, but the work of educators committed to supporting children's relationships and pursuits—and to deepening their own relationships and understandings, as well. This book is instruction for educators: not to buy heaps of cups for your classroom, in the hope of reconstructing this investigation, but to keep close watch for small acts of magic, and when they appear, to live boldly into these verbs.

It is also potent instruction for people who don't spend their days with children: listen beyond "*children say the darnedest things,*" look below the stacking and bashing, and your understanding of children's capacities and educators' work will be transformed. This little gem of a book offers insight into the purpose of education beyond alphabet drills and counting skills; it expands our thinking about the teaching and learning process.

The story of the children, the educators, the families, and the cups embodies the conviction that education both requires and nurtures imagination, determination, vision, humility, experimentation, relationship, and listening. Bridgette, Angela, the children, and their families demonstrate the generosity, playfulness, and intellectual vitality of a community anchored by these qualities—a community alive with small acts of magic.

*Ann Pelo* and *Margie Carter*
Editors of the *Reimagining Our Work* (ROW) Collection
Authors of *From Teaching to Thinking: A Pedagogy for Reimagining Our Work*

# introduce

Kids' Domain Early Learning Centre is a full time early childhood education centre in Auckland, New Zealand. The charitable society under which Kids' Domain operates was established in 1985 to provide on-site quality childcare for the children of families who work on the Auckland City Hospital campus in Grafton. From the outside it appears to be a very ordinary place, but venture within, and a learning community of wonder and discovery opens up before your eyes.

Over a period of time Kids' Domain has been building a community of inquiry that reflects the bicultural values and principles of early childhood education in Aotearoa New Zealand. As we live and breathe these values and principles in our practice we have become increasingly aware of the importance and value of children and adults being curious together as researchers.

This book tells the story of the experiences of the learning community in Tūmanako— the four-year-old room—researching together over an extended 18 month period. It tells of the extraordinary encounters between everyday plastic cups, children, teachers, parents and extended family/whānau, and the innovative and significant learning that was generated.

It is my pleasure to introduce this book to you, and to acknowledge and thank the children, teachers, parents, and extended family members whose work is represented in it.

I also thank the Kids' Domain governance group and parent community for trusting us to move beyond the known into places of unknowing and gladly committing valuable resources of time and money into this work.

Immense thanks to Bridgette Towle for her pedagogical leadership and insightful facilitation of this inquiry. Your presence and writing has inspired us to wonder together about the vital role materials play in children's learning. Thanks also to Angela Heape who has helped Bridgette sift and sort through thousands of images, video clips, teacher notes, and documents to bring the voices of children and their thinking alive, and to bring to birth the story of the cup.

*Julianne Exton*
Director, Kids' Domain Early Learning Centre

# preface

The cup crept softly into our lives; an unexpected visitor. At first we didn't think much of it, and then slowly, over time, it drew us deeper and deeper into encounter, continually challenging and provoking us to look and think differently.

The cup opened our eyes to the power and force of "things" and their ability to affect creative expression, and the construction of knowledge. Time and again we bore witness to phenomenal and jaw-dropping occurrences.

Who would have thought exchanges between four-year-olds and simple plastic cups would result in such intricate, creative building designs? Structures were sculptural, from the ethereally fairy-tale, to the solid and imposing.

Who would have thought that cups could be the catalyst of inquiry and theory making, naturally entangling the discrete disciplines of math, science, literacy, and digital technology? Learning was contextual, situated, connected, and holistic, and constantly flowing in a processual movement generating new ways of being and knowing.

Who would have thought that cups could break down social barriers and act as agents for inclusion and relationship building? Forging unlikely alliances between children who weren't particularly friends with one another: girls built with boys; old hands included new children. The cups reached out to draw materials, places, children, teachers, and families into relationship as a community of researchers and innovators.

Te Whāriki, the New Zealand early childhood curriculum, emphasises a holistic, interconnected approach to learning based on children's "reciprocal and responsive relationships with *people, places and things*."[1] Our experiences with cups flipped this around to bring *"things"* to the fore. The cups shifted our gaze to reconceptualise the vital role materials, objects, and artefacts play as powerful participants in interactive, interconnected learning experiences.

This book tells the story of the cup phenomenon. It has been written for our learning community to document and celebrate our joyful adventure into new ways of imagining and knowing the world. We hope it will be revisited and treasured by all for years to come.

The book has also been written to share with educators, and anyone else who may be interested in the way children, teachers, and families live and learn in relationship with the material world. We see the universe as interconnected and interdependent and believe it is vitally important for educators to share their experiences and thinking with one another. When this happens, we can collectively evolve pedagogical practice in ways that potentiate new possible futures and realities based on an ethics of care, difference, and mutual relation with all who inhabit and comprise Earth.

Our intention is to make visible our thinking, questioning, decision making, and the insights we gained as we marvelled, listened, and experimented together during this emergent inquiry. We want to go beyond simply offering an account of our experience and invite you to think and question along with us. As you read we encourage you to pay attention to what connections, thoughts, and sensations are evoked in you. Perhaps you will question your own relationship with material things, and how it is possible to set aside predetermined outcomes to move *with* others in an emergent flow of events that is uncertain, and open to invention and creativity of thought.

Our perspectives are influenced and inspired by the work of Ann Pelo and Margie Carter. We thank them enormously for their generous support, and for challenging and encouraging us to give stronger consideration and voice to our role as pedagogical thinkers, facilitators, and inquirers.

We invite you to enter into our realm of wonder and discovery, and into encounter with the cup for yourself. We hope it will reach out to touch and affect you too.


*Bridgette Towle* and *Angela Heape*

# arrive

On a cold mid-winter's day Ira arrived with a desire. He'd seen YouTube videos of people speed stacking plastic cups and was keen to experiment for himself. It is important to us to support children's investigative urges as we believe they naturally generate authentic discovery and learning, so we went with Ira to the kitchen to find some plastic cups and the building began.

We noticed that Ira didn't race straight into speed stacking as we had expected; he took his time to familiarise himself with the qualities and affordances of the cups.

First he placed the cups face up to form a base. This produced stability issues for the next layer so he turned them over to face down. With a more reliable foundation, Ira started experimenting with tower-like structures.

Crashes became an inevitable part of the experimentation process and with each new construction Ira's concentration and precision increased.

Captivated by the growing intensity we willed Ira on as he slowly and carefully layered one cup on top of another to test how tall he could build a single vertical tower. As the stakes of the build increased so did the tension in the air. Suddenly, taut energy erupted into expressions of joy or frustration as Ira danced from foot to foot to celebrate a successful addition, or stamped in protest at the cups' collapse.

# spread

The buzz from Ira's engagement with the cups spread quickly across the room. His enthusiasm was like a contagion compelling others to enter into encounter with these "ordinary" everyday objects.

Over the next few days the cups went "viral." Children fed off each other's experimentation and rejoiced together at the marvel of new configurations.

The rapid demand for cups soon outstripped our supplies. A momentum was building and we wanted to ensure that the children had ample resources to fully explore their emerging ideas. We needed more cups and fast!

We began to wonder what would happen if we introduced the element of colour. In what ways would this new dimension affect the children's interactions with the cups?

With anticipation we introduced vivid red, green, and blue cups.

Immediately we saw that the new cups' vibrant colour and translucency amplified their call for encounter.

The children answered their call, working fervently, alone and in groups, delving deeper into the possibilities and potential of the cups. We called it...

*the cup craze*

# construct

The children's voracious experimentation with cups afforded a natural exploration of mathematical and geometric concepts.

The initial interest in simple single towers quickly evolved into triangular configurations, and we wondered if this was driven by the children's desire to create larger, taller, and more stable constructions.

Coloured cups offered opportunities for sorting, matching, grouping, and patterning. Colours were often classified; clumped together, layered, or arranged in algebraic patterns to make aesthetically pleasing colour schemes.

*Exploration of shape, line, and form became extensive.*

Once the triangular configuration was struck upon, the concept of "speed cup stacking" was revisited. This really tested the children's agility and powers of concentration.

To add another layer of complexity to the game Jack struck upon the idea of using a triangle as a measuring device. With each beat of the triangle Jack counted out loud so the others could track their progress and compare times.

The children's discovery of how to construct corners and curves gave rise to the most spectacular and intricate three-dimensional forms; the tubular and spiral tower.

The stability of tubular towers enabled the children to fully explore the dimension of height.

Let's build it really big, right up to the clouds! Nate

The ladder won't reach to the clouds so we'll just build up to the roof. Cooper

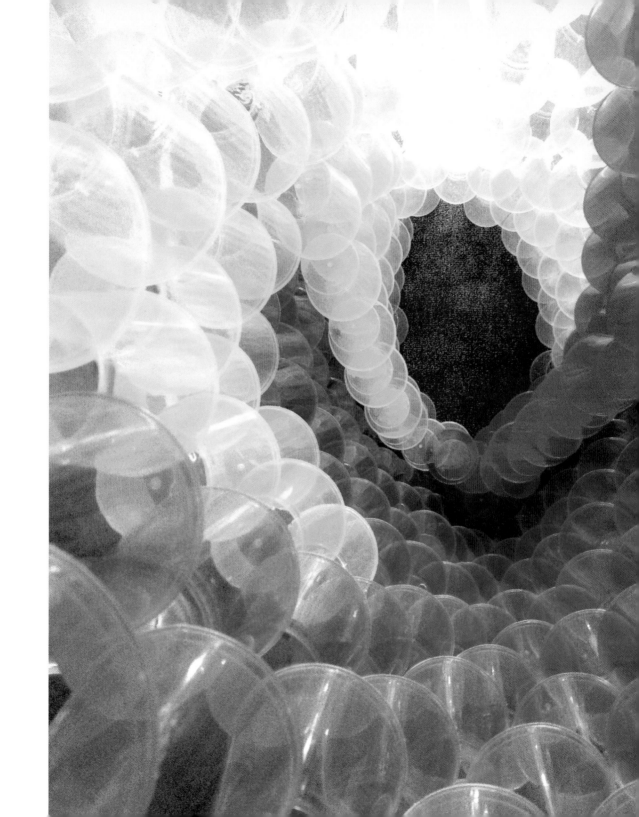

patterning

sorting

locating

counting

grouping

classifying

measuring

comparing

sequencing

estimating

proportioning

balancing

stabilising

increasing

dividing

repeating

The "cup craze" was affecting us as much as the children. As we listened, observed, and participated in the unfolding events our sensitivity to the force of materials as agents in the children's creative learning processes was being activated and enlivened. Our curiosity aroused, we began noticing the children incorporating other elements into their constructions. In response, we offered them additional materials and objects to experiment with including fabrics, numbers, and loose parts such as sticks and cardboard tubes. We also offered miniature cups and large plastic buckets. We thought carefully about how we could set the conditions for autonomous and open-ended experimentation that could provoke new threads of thinking and creative possibilities.

The children's cup constructions became increasingly complex. Wooden blocks became a feature opening up a whole new aspect of building potential. We began to see incredible feats of engineering to overcome obstacles such as structures climbing stairs. We saw children balancing cups precariously on top of blocks, or using them as a decorative feature, to give the buildings another added dimension.

The process of building had no constraints and was as important as the final product. Often children engaged in lengthy storytelling and imaginative play and games as they placed their components. For some, wholehearted immersion in the unfolding, dynamic realms of imaginary and elaborate fantasy play was far more desirable than creating a representative construction.

# transform

One day an unexpected event led to new wonder and discovery. Ira arrived and all of the cups were being used by other children. This seemed like an opportune time to invite Ira to create a plan; a "design map" for his building while he waited for his turn. The intertwined process of thinking and drawing can be a powerful generator of ideas and a chance to make visible working theories. The culture of drawing, thinking, and design mapping has grown in our centre over time and we often use the quiet contemplative space of the studio for this concentrated work.

Using black pen on paper Ira completed a beautiful diagram of intricate lines. "*It's a big airplane which transforms into a big castle when it lands.*"

We hung Ira's plan on the studio wall and he constantly referred to it as he assembled the cups.

Colours were carefully chosen, blue first. An organic line was made and then filled in. Ira added red cups and gave it a three-dimensional aspect with a tower in the middle. Green cups extended the shape; it was beginning to look remarkably like his plan.

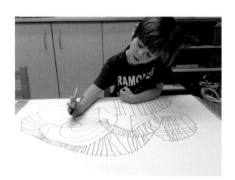

Ira displayed incredible skill in transferring his two-dimensional plan to a "real life" three-dimensional structure.

As Ira stood contemplating his work he thought aloud: "*If the light was off it would glow out everywhere behind you.*"

Ira switched off the light to test his theory. Much to his delight the cups indeed appeared to glow. Fired by this discovery Ira asked if we could block out all the natural light to see if the cups glowed brighter.

Our instinctive response was to support and accompany Ira in his investigations. To encourage children to take risks and be inventive it is important to think genuinely alongside them about what might be possible, rather than steering them towards the "right" answer, or toward our own predetermined ideas. As teachers we want to model that we can embrace uncertainty, be playful, and willing to experiment in the moment.

Together we found and fixed blankets and sheets over the windows and door. Ira switched off the light again. This time he discovered that without any light they didn't glow at all.

Initially disappointed, Ira paused to think some more. A new idea struck; torches could shine light and make the cups glow! Fuelled by excitement we scoured the centre and found a couple of torches, a few tea lights, and a green floodlight.

Ira experimented again.

An encounter between materials, child, and teacher generated transformational affect eliciting a sense of curiosity, surprise, and enchanting creativity.

One material had beckoned another material, and in their meeting they melded together to become a singular sculptural entity. Light passed by and through plastic cups taking something of them along with it while leaving traces of itself behind. The energy of cup-light radiated outwards infusing the space to "glow out everywhere behind you," and through you, just as Ira had imagined.

It felt as if the protagonists, human and non-human, had taken on a new dimension; a new quality of life in an entangled world of possibilities and potential.

In this profound moment of beauty and grace the light studio was born.

The aesthetic effect produced by combining lights with cups captured the hearts, minds, and bodies of children and teachers alike. Inspired by this unexpected change in events we decided to set up an immersive space that opened up deeper possibilities of investigation.

The light studio, newly festooned with an array of potential light sources, coloured cups, paper, and pens, offered a peaceful and provocative space where children could take time to contemplate and create.

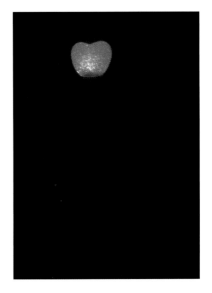

The added dimension of light afforded more complex design possibilities and effects. Charlotte carefully studied the lighting options before decisively drawing a "cup castle" plan that included light fixtures. Charlotte worked methodically, pausing often to soak in the detail of her plan. When Charlotte placed the heart light on top of her castle tower she turned off the studio lights to check the effect. She was ecstatic with the illusion of the heart light floating in mid-air. Torches and tea lights were added and the final construction checked in darkness. Charlotte was dissatisfied with the end result realising that the added lights diminished the impact of the glowing heart. Charlotte's aesthetic sensibility propelled her to turn off the superfluous lighting to embrace the unexpected, mystical effect of a floating, glowing heart.

*Materials seem to have their own inner life and their own story to tell. Yet they can only be transformed through their encounter with people.*

–Lella Gandini and Judith Allen Kaminsky[2]

# inspire

By coincidence, the Auckland Art Gallery was hosting an international exhibition of light art, shortly after light had emerged as a transforming energy in the children's experimentation with the cups.

We were curious to see how different immersive and multisensory experiences with light would affect the children's thinking and creativity.

We visited the exhibition in small groups to experience artworks that explored colour, intensity, and projection of light.

This was a wonder-filled interactive experience where atmospheric installations and intangible sculptures could be moved around and through. Being immersed within the energy of an artistic illusion played with our senses and perceptions. This inspired us to offer the children lights in different configurations that could be used at varying heights and angles.

On return to the studio, new strings of flickering lights hanging from overhead wires and flashing snake-like cords, afforded a sense of movement and increased vitality to the children's creations.

# collaborate

Amy and Anjali decided that they wanted to collaborate on a cup building together in the studio. They began with a plan, a collaborative drawing that unfolded as ideas flowed, collided, and merged.

Each drew a figure, and then together, a tall tower-like structure. Watching each other intently they took turns to draw doors and windows.

There can be two doors, one little door for her kitty, and a big door for her.

Anjali

With the plan complete and hung on the wall to guide their building the girls began to explore the lights and the possibilities they presented.

They discovered delicate strings of fairy lights that flickered in soft hues of pink, blue, and white. Captured by their ethereality, the girls soon began a game of catching a colour between their fingers before it magically disappeared to re-emerge elsewhere.

The girls considered the entire studio space in the design of their construction. A long rope of flashing coloured lights was wound artistically around the outer edge of the room. A white LED spotlight, enveloped in pink cellophane, was fixed to the floor as a centrepiece for the tower.

A column quickly rose from the circular foundation of their building. A piece of cardboard was inserted to form a lintel for the window; a vital component to the structure!

The girls' approach to the construction reflected their personal preferences and learning styles. Anjali was happy to freely mix the colours for a rainbow effect, Amy preferred a more ordered approach, using one batch of colours at a time.

Moments of silent, companionable engagement were frequently punctuated with bursts of chatter, giggles at mishaps, and inventive game playing.

Look at this, I can still talk! Amy

This is really
beautiful! It
makes all the
room pink!

Anjali

With the build complete, attention was turned to the strategic placement of fairy lights from overhead wires.

The finished structure was a marvel to behold and the girls took turns with the iPad, capturing images from every angle.

The children have been enthusiastic and intuitive photographers. We found it fascinating to observe their choice of perspective, what captures their attention, and what they believe is representative of their encounter.

The photos on the following pages have been taken by the children. They are a glimpse into a different point of view; a point of view with a striking focus on detail.

*photographs taken by children...*

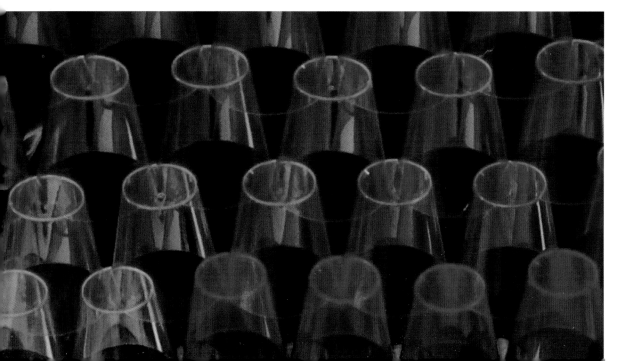

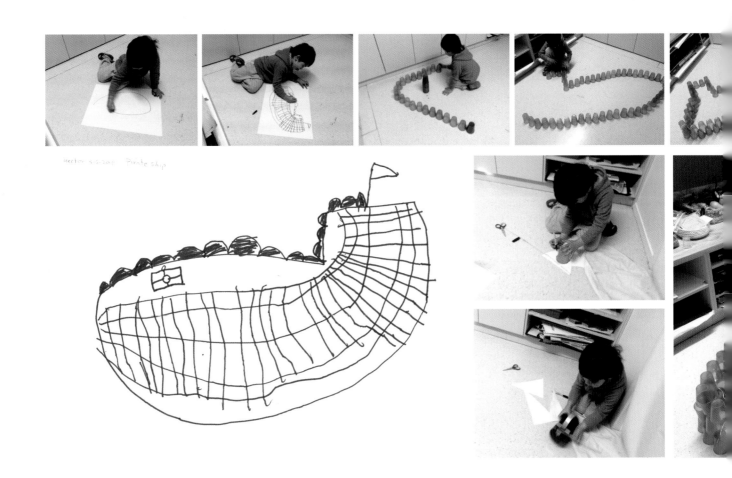

Hector's ... Pirate ship

*Construction and imagination, two linked worlds and languages that children always keep closely together in their knowledge building strategies.*

–Reggio Children[3]

# storytelling

Naturally entangled in the worlds of construction and imagination is the language of storytelling. Encounters between children, cups, and lights opened a portal to fantastical worlds generating stories of adventure and mystery. Storytelling sparked new connections and relationships between ideas, theories, things, people, and places—real and imagined! The children's narratives showed us how powerful materials and objects are as activators of expressive storytelling and metaphoric thinking: both important components of literacy learning. Alert to the richness unfolding before us, we listened and scribed the children's stories, and in doing so, showed them how much we believe in their capabilities as creative thinkers and storytellers.

*The Witch and the Princess*

*The witch wanted to take the princess away from her rainbow castle. The witch thought the castle was lovely and she wanted it for herself. The witch wasn't allowed any lovely stuff and this made her angry. The witch built her castle beside the princess castle so she could creep in the night to get the princess. One night the witch got in the top and came down the chimney, 'cause the door was locked, and 'cause the prince forgot to lock the chimney! The witch was trying to get the princess to take her away but there was a magic necklace around the witch's neck and the princess cut it in half and the witch's hair turned grey and her necklace fell off. It made her even wickeder! The princess doesn't get taken away. The princess cuts the apple in half and the witch eats it and turns into the ground—there's just her cape and her hat left. They turn into the princess's daddy! He'd been in the witch's necklace for a long time. It was magic. The witch sang a little song and he disappeared into her necklace! The princess was so happy to see her Daddy again.*

By Daniel C

Back In the main construction area we noticed the children's constructions were increasingly representing "real" buildings and elements from their own personal experiences.

### this is the city

### this is the Sky Tower

We wondered if a monochromatic colour scheme could help represent the children's real life experiences and extend their ideas and understandings. Would a different colour scheme also change their practice of building?

We introduced black and white cups and we couldn't resist experimenting with them ourselves first. The cups were calling directly to us now and it was time to tune into their frequency; to listen at skin level! Coming up against the force of the cups was unexpectedly challenging and we became even more appreciative of the children's building skills.

The new cups were taken up with great enthusiasm by the children who noticed that they were just the right size to stack up the steps.

With the bright colours taken away, the children played with form.
Curves and swirls appeared and the "diamond" configuration of
placing the cups rim to rim became a popular way to top the towers.

# investigate

The children's interests when they built with the cups still primarily involved buildings from their own experience, mixed up with elements from their imaginations.

We wondered what would happen if we went out into our immediate community and investigated the buildings there. Would this inform and influence what they knew about buildings? What new potential connections and possibilities might this open up in their experimentations and thinking?

Carparks were an especially popular building choice amongst the boys, so we focused on the Auckland Hospital carpark, along with other Hospital buildings, when we embarked on a series of research field trips.

The small groups would firstly stop and gaze at the Auckland City skyline. We would count the cranes and speculate whether the buildings were all attached or stood alone. Moving on, in amongst the Hospital buildings, we would examine all sorts of interesting features, the shape and height of buildings, bridges spanning between buildings, and other curiosities like vents and chimneys.

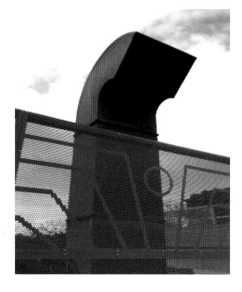

The new carpark building's exterior was intriguing and so we took some time to consider its mesh curves and tree-patterned texture.

Inside the carpark, the children took note of everything they could see.

There were prominent numbers in different colours, signs, arrows, lines, and wheelchair markings. The ramps were a huge source of interest as we watched cars go up and down and make their way around the carpark.

After the walks, we invited the children into the studio to recap and discuss what they had seen.

They were then invited to draw any aspects that had impressed them.

*The chimney looks like a long stick. The lines on the ladder are for the children to climb. A big carpark, holes on the wall.*

Emma

*I'm gonna do the buildings, with the hospital and the other buildings. This is the bridge. They're the stripes on the bridge. I'm gonna draw some persons.*

Anjali

*I can see trees, tree branches.*

Aidan

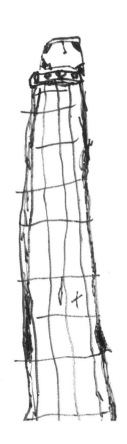

*That's the chimney that makes the clouds.* Aidan

*The chimney is wobbly.* Finau

*When you go further away, it looks like it's falling.* Xavier

*It seems like it's going to fall on us.* Georgia

It became very apparent to us that our walks had influenced the children's ideas and building process. Elements from what they saw on the walks began appearing in their constructions. Numbers, such as we had seen on the walls of the carpark, were well utilised. Ramps and entrances were common features and the cars were often placed in their own carparks.

It's a whole big city hospital! It has some gates and locks. Max

It has some cars to park inside the carpark. Gabriel

Mine's getting taller and taller. You need to stack it well so it doesn't fall over. I'm building the big carpark and it's not gonna fall.

Harry

# reflect

The environment became filled with our investigation. Surfaces acted as mirrors, reflecting back to the children their experiences, thinking, and inventions; recasting them for further interpretation and elaboration.

It was our intention to infuse the room with the life of the inquiry; to see what happened when documentation and artefacts are treated as protagonists for learning in and of themselves. We projected video footage and images of walks in the Hospital grounds on the wall as children actively experimented. Instead of filing drawings away they became artefacts: transportable objects that could be handled, moved, discussed, and even incorporated into structures.

It was important for us that the children be active participants in this process. We encouraged and assisted them to become documenters and assessors of their own work. Children photographed, selected, printed, and posted large, bold images of their cup buildings on the wall to revisit and share with others.

Drawings and images made visible the multiplicity of children's different ideas and interpretations. They acted as provocateurs to look anew, to consider other, more expansive, ways of thinking and doing.

Documentation became active and alive: alive with a movement and force in itself to affect new potentialities and possibilities.

Everyone is in the city. The shops, people standing waiting for the Sky Tower, a fire engine, a car centre, and a hospital.

Sophie

The reflective and collective space of the construction area prompted more collaborative drawing and building. The children were keen to reiterate their thinking and design mapping so we provided drawing materials for them to work with.

Here, a group of children each drew their own elements before working individually to bring them to life. It was interesting to note the marked renaissance of the blocks in this building event, with only a nod to the use of cups.

This is Kids' Domain. This is Centre 1, Centre 2, and Centre 3.

Harry

I built the Harbour Bridge, 'cause we go on the Harbour Bridge to go to Kids' Domain.

Nate

I like the carpark 'cause I've been there and 'cause it has holes in it so I can see inside there.

Aidan

Then, all in agreement, they decided to attach their buildings to one another, in order to make them "bigger."

# It's the whole of Auckland City!

Cooper

# attach

We can attach it to everyone's
building—like a spider's web!

Lucas

Over many months of cup building we noticed the emergence of a group "lingo" or special vocabulary between children to describe particular phenomena such as "attach" and "bash," "diamond" and "three-on-three."

The word "attach" seemed to refer to an intriguing phenomenon that saw tentacle-like arms of cups or blocks reaching in and out of buildings as if seeking connection with others.

When the environment was buzzing with construction, particularly first thing in the morning, the desire to "attach" structures to others was particularly evident. We were intrigued. What was driving this urge to attach buildings? We began wondering if there was an association between the physical attachment of buildings and children's social interactions, and their sense of belonging to the group. We decided to listen more carefully to see if we could gain deeper insight into the children's perspectives.

We heard children theorising that attaching buildings makes them *"big and long,"* stronger and more durable. *"If everybody attaches their building together it will be humungous"* and *"we'll be able to keep it for two nights!"* It also appeared that an attached building took on the qualities of the strongest one in the group and was less likely to "bash."

This physical or material aspect of attachment seemed to exist in parallel to the social and emotional interactions between the children. There seemed to be an awareness of strength in solidarity and children were eager to invite or seek attachment. At times we heard lengthy negotiations of who could attach whose building to whose. Occasionally, these negotiations weren't always democratic and children struggled with the injustice of being excluded. As the children worked through these difficulties we saw and felt the emergence of an effervescent energy; an excitement that burst into moments of joy and jubilation as they discovered the potential of being inclusive and joining forces.

We could build an enormous one with all
the cups, all together.
It will be awesome if we do it all together!

Ira

We saw the children transfer and apply their understanding of "attachment" to their ventures out in the hospital grounds. They seemed fascinated with the bridges or tunnels connecting or "attaching" buildings. Nate said the bridge is so *"you can go from building to building to visit friends."*

A growing awareness of buildings existing in relationship to others was enriching the children's constructions and we began to notice a surge of increasingly elaborate "attaching" structures.

The children's thinking was broadening. Attention was shifting beyond individual design and "attachment" to the aesthetic effect and functionality of an entire city of buildings.

Spaces between buildings became important. We noticed children grappling with the dilemma of wanting to attach structures, while also allowing space to be able to move in, and around them.

This is the city. It's all attached.

All of them are attached. Hector

One day a surprising event led to a spine-tingling revelation about the complexity of the children's perception of attachment.

Nate was lying on his tummy drawing people on a piece of paper in the construction area surrounded by a small group of friends. As Nate drew, he and his friends talked about how the friends and family in his picture were all "attached." It was as if the boys were linking their cup construction experiences and ideas about cities to their social interactions and sense of family and community.

Seeing this unexpected exchange between Nate and his friends provided insight into the depth of children's understanding around the notion of attachment, and the apparent ease in which they move between the realms of concrete and abstract ways of knowing. On a physical "concrete" level attachment meant making buildings stronger, taller, and more elaborate. Attention needs to be given to "spaces in-between" in order to function well as a whole. On a social and emotional "abstract" level attachment meant connecting to others, being in relationship, and belonging to something bigger than oneself.

*Attention needs to be given to 'spaces in-between' in order to function well as a whole.*

The children seemed to naturally view this thing they called "attaching" from an interconnected, holistic perspective and we were left wondering if there may be other elements to their awareness and understanding that in our "adultness" we were unable to consciously perceive. This left us pondering many "big" questions.

As we grow into adulthood, why, and how, does our understanding of the world become so fragmented?

What do we miss if we organise and compartmentalise our thoughts into fixed ways of seeing and thinking?

From a teaching perspective, how does fragmented thinking affect our practice?

If children naturally synthesise physical, cognitive, emotional, and social ways of knowing then why do we identify and assess these separately?

Does focusing on the individual channel our vision away from relationships connecting the whole?

Loris Malaguzzi speaks of the ubiquity of interdependence and we wonder what more we might discover if we broaden our gaze to look for the connections, in-between ways of knowing, ideas, places, people, and things:

*Think of interconnecting, the great verb of the present and the future. A great verb we must be capable of understanding deep down, and of conjugating as part of our hard work; bearing in mind that we live in a world no longer made of islands, but in a world made of webs. In this image there is the construction of children's thinking and the construction of our own thinking. A construction that cannot be made up of islands that are separate, but which belong to a great archipelago, to a great web, in which interference, interaction, inter-disciplinarity is the constant, even when we cannot see it, even when we think it doesn't exist, or that it isn't there.  Interdependence is there.*

–Loris Malaguzzi[4]

# connect

Alert to the complex interconnections at play during cup-child encounters we began to notice that some family members were very attentive to the cup phenomenon and lingered in the mornings to experiment for themselves. This made us curious and we began to wonder what learning might be generated if the children and their families could experience building with the cups together at home. We wondered how the families' experiences might compare with ours, and how any differences or similarities may affect future events.

So, with the hope of discovering more about the "cup" as a vessel of potential and possibility, we invited families to take home a humungous bag of white cups to experiment with. There were no rules, limitations, or expectations. All we asked is that families capture some of their experiences on camera and feed back to us their thoughts about the cups as a material to experiment and play with.

*Some of the best moments were when the stack of cups crashed to the floor! At first, the girls would be frustrated or disappointed, but they would then work out another way to try again and problem solve.*

The Hyde Family

*We learnt how much fun it was to build high towers and then smash them down. We made a really tall tower and then made a video of the smash. It was so much fun playing it in slow motion, then playing it backwards!*

The Oti Family

*Talia took the lead and Chloe wanted to assist. Chloe was living through Talia's excitement.*

The Svirskis Family

*Different people interacted with the cups differently. The kids were far less worried about defects in the cups, in the pattern of the building and even when it collapses. Adults were quick to discard certain cups with damage, attempt to realign the cup spacing, or get annoyed when it knocked down. Adults tend to 'build until collapse' but the kids were satisfied to call it complete sooner.*

The Dryland Family

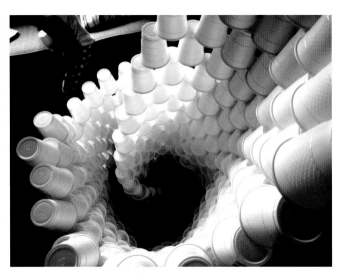
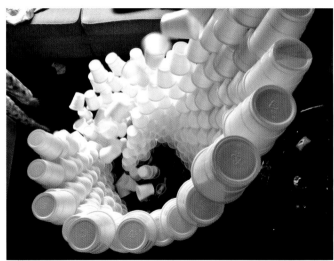

The Hyde Family

*Sally and I had the same idea of what to build. We don't think Nate had thought about incorporating something into the structure. But when he understood what we wanted to do he was all for it.*

The Hollis Family

We were amazed by the families' inventiveness and listening to their feedback we could identify experiences that were common to our own:

- working together means building faster and higher;

- open communication is vitally important when working collaboratively;

- children competently lead and infect others with their knowledge and enthusiasm;

- different people interact with the cups differently—some are concerned with order, pattern, or form, whereas others are more experimental and playful;

- symmetry and form make buildings stronger;

- iconic and familiar structures can be highly influential;

- realising your vision requires patience, persistence, and precision; and finally

- the extraordinary sensation of disappointment and exhilaration that surges through your body as you watch your building collapse.

Most importantly, the families' enterprising and courageous experimentation opened our minds to new possibilities. When the height of the Dryland family's cup building was constrained by their ceiling they moved their cup construction work outside to the farm shed. Some families incorporated substantial objects, furniture, and even animals into their cup structures!

We also noticed children seemed to use their bodies more forcefully and freely in their interactions with the cups. The images show children thrilling in the sensation of kicking and running at, and through the cups to cause collapse.

The families' experiences left us stimulated and inspired. We were now thinking more deeply about the way materials and ordinary everyday "things" have the ability to speak to adults and children alike. The cups seemed to possess an alluring connective force that drew children, families, teachers, places, concepts, and ideas into collective experimentation. This made us reflect on how the majority of commercial toys are one-dimensional and unable to induce such rich relational learning and creative invention.

# bash

Throughout the cup phenomenon we witnessed the challenge and artistry of tall cup towers and beautiful sculptures giving way to the theatre and brilliance of their inevitable collapse. The children named this infuriating, disappointing, yet spectacular and enthralling event a "bash."

Children became intimately aware of how cups act, singularly and in unison. They developed an intuitive awareness of the cups' subtlest movements. It was as if they were tuned into a living body that moved and pulsated; sensitive to the latent energy ready to burst forth at any time. The moment cups "explode" into life, time stands still. It is as if the cups are demanding you to listen to them; it is their turn to lead.

In this timeless space you stand mesmerised, captivated by the vibrancy and force of the cups as they reach out and peel away. Limbs frozen, only your face expresses the sensation of exhilaration resonating throughout your being. For a moment it seems as if boundaries between cup, child, and teacher become blurred.

Every "bash" is utterly unique. The sound, speed, and sequence can be explosive, or almost conversational in its rhythms and pauses. Buildings may dramatically implode in an instant, falling as one entity, or slowly peel away, layer by layer, cup by cup, as if in a flamboyant, choreographed dance.

It's like a volcano erupting and that's the lava. It's erupting like a volcano.

Harry

It's like a water fountain, a water fountain falling.

Tia

The children talked passionately about cup "bashes." It was like they were caught in a game with the cups; a test of wills. This made us wonder how the children perceived agency in their relationship with the cups. Did the children or the cups hold the power, or is it in a constant state of flux? We listened attentively to learn more about the children's thoughts and strategies.

We heard a wide range of theories and thought this presented an opportunity to extend and challenge thinking. We decided to create a group forum where the children could exchange thoughts and consider different points of view. We were curious to see how thinking as a collective potentiated new possibilities.

We recorded the "build and bash" of a cup building and replayed it in slow motion at a group meeting time for analysis and discussion.

The following dialogue illustrates the diversity of opinion among the children and the degree of hypothesising and testing that was happening. It also provides an intriguing insight into the children's perspective of "things" as powerful and agentic, and as capable of working in concert with, or against one another to produce effects.

*Thing power: the curious ability of inanimate things to animate, to act, to produce effects dramatic and subtle.*

–Jane Bennett[5]

*It's the diamonds, maybe because of the diamonds.* Harry

*Maybe the diamond was too wobbly on top of the other diamond.* Emily

*The black cup fell onto the white cup.* Harry

*The black cups are heavier than the white cups, the white cups are not heavier.* Levi

*Maybe the black cups are bigger and the white cups are smaller.* Xavier

*They are both the same. They're the same size but different colours.*
*I know because I've tested them both in buildings.* Aidan

*Black cups are stronger.* Hector

*Maybe all the white cups were wobbly.* Tia

*The white cups are lighter.* Anjali

*Well, I agree with Anjali.* Daniel

*I don't agree with Anjali. The ladder moved and bashed the cups.* Harry

*Maybe the black cups bumped the white cups and it came on a lean and it bashed.* Aidan

*I think I saw a baby outside so he come inside and maybe bashed the building.* Levi

*No! There were no babies in there.* Collective

*I saw a baby outside though.* Levi

# theorise

Children continued to share theories about why and how buildings "bash." A lingo emerged to describe potential causes and culprits such as the "diamond," "two-on-two," and "three-on-three." Daniel explains "two-on-two" as "...*one cup is in another cup and it bashes because it's too lumpy and too thick.*"

Wooden blocks were regarded by some children as a far more reliable building material and preferred to construct cup buildings on a solid wooden foundation, "*cups are soft, wood is hard.*" Eva thought cups are softer and less reliable because they are plastic, "*I think it's because the cups are plastic. You know how we put plastic things in bins—maybe the cups are plastic. They're soft and they're too smooth.*" Emily sided with the cups, "*cups don't want to fall down, it is the blocks that make them fall down.*"

Cups were attributed qualities that determined their strength and durability according to their size and colour, "*black cups are heavier and stronger, white cups are weaker and lighter.*"

Some children theorised that building shape and height affects the cups stability and can cause "*jiggling*," "*wobbling*," and "*tilting*" that may, or may not, lead to collapse—"*My one's leaning, but it didn't bash. It wobbled but it didn't bash!*"

*A broken cup—look, a crack, it's going to make my building fall.*
Tia

*It's a complicated building. We started with the blocks but the cups bashed it so we started again.*
Aidan

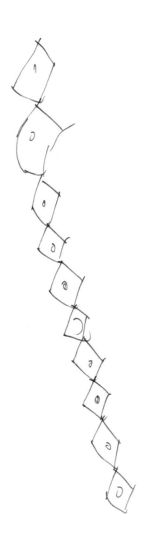

*A diamond with a light inside, and then another diamond and then it gets too tall and it bashes. Look it is leaning!*
Tia

The children were continually evolving and refining their theories and we began to see building techniques to lessen the likelihood of collapse, *"we're only doing three diamonds 'cause it's starting to wobble."*

Having experimented with analysing cup "bashes" at half speed in a large group, we wondered what might be revealed when the children analysed even slower video footage with the ability to pause playback to discuss their ideas. Using slow motion exposed extraordinary images that provoked animated dialogue. Previously unseen detail led to theories that now appraised not only the cause of collapse, but the flow and flight of collapse. Children were beginning to move from *why* buildings bash to *how*.

During the session we offered the children pen and paper. Drawing while thinking and theorising can provide opportunity to clarify ideas and work through inconsistencies. Drawing makes thinking visible to others and invites engagement that can lead to an enriched exchange and intermingling of ideas.[6]

*I'm going to do the cups first. And now the 'crookeds' at the top. Now I want to do it when it's bashing.*

Finau

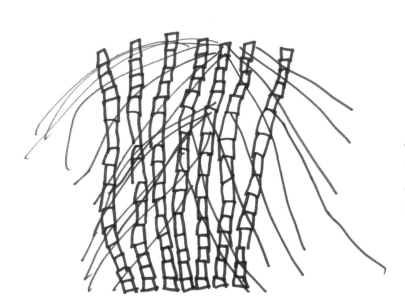

*See these cups falling down, they're tipping over. Look, it's falling! The cups go falling down in lines.*

Eva

We view children as intelligent and intuitive and believe that if we ask thoughtful questions out of genuine curiosity, and provide conditions for expansive thinking, then children's imaginative theorising will flow. The complexity of the mental images that materialise constantly enthral and intrigue us.

Anjali exaggerated the edges of the cups to illustrate the root cause of a "bash"; however, as her drawing evolved it became apparent that the edges acted in concert with the element of height, and the precarious "diamond" configuration, to cause collapse. Interestingly, it is the upper hand of the human who casts the final blow "to make sure it falls."

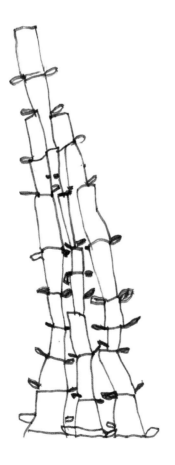

*I think the reason why it's bashing down is because of the little bits that are sticking out—the edges.*

*So one cup is on it and it makes it too tall, then it's tilting, and then it's going to look like it's falling down.*

*I'm going to do a diamond so it actually looks like it's coming down—to make sure it falls.*
Anjali

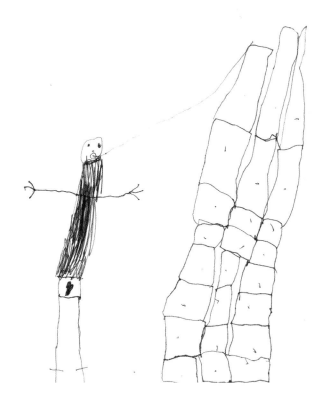

*That's me blowing at my building and it's going to fall. It's going to fall on that spot!*
Talia

Talia's drawing and theorising reveals an intimate awareness of how cup buildings behave. She seems able to predict the exact spot on which it will fall. Again, it was interesting to note that it was the human casting the determining blow—this time literally!

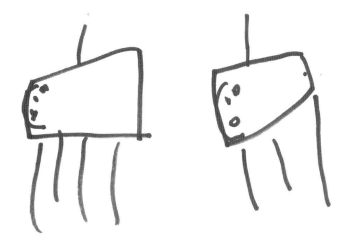

*I'm going to draw some legs and some eyes on my cup and he's going to be fast.*

*There he's creeping and there he's running. He's running to the building and he's going to knock it all over and then they are going to bash down.*

Emily

Emily's thinking is different. Emily crosses the ontological divide between humans and non-humans to anthropomorphise the cup. Emily attributes her cup with human-like qualities to portray "him" as an animated and self-determining being. Emily's cup acts independently and intentionally to mount a sneak attack on the cup building. First he creeps... and then he runs!

Emily imagines and expresses a world that does not see humans as separated, outside of, or above non-human things; instead, Emily sees cups as part of an interconnected and interdependent world where entities morph and merge in relationship with one another. This reminds us that children are migrant thinkers not yet constrained by the orthodox organising principles of adulthood.

Perhaps children's ability to see the world as a relational whole, rather than as fragmented, leaves them open to the vital life force of everyday things, and more easily able to discern the extraordinary in the ordinary.[7]

If children can be more attuned to the enchanting vitality of material things how can we learn from, and with them, so we can reconnect to our latent ability to sense the energetic life in non-human matter? How can we give "the force of things more due" in our pedagogical work with the children?[8]

These questions linger in our minds and can only be answered as we continue to live and learn in entangled relationship with others.

# embody

In exploration and play children come to know "things" not by focusing on what they *are* but what they can *do*.

Children openly explored the potential of the cups through interacting with them using their entire bodies. Interactions between cup and child generated knowledge about their own body, the cup, and what happens when they join forces. Each affected the other's being; transforming senses, appearances, and identities.

Embodying the essence of the cup, "becoming with" the cup, was an interconnected, dynamic process; a process that saw a constant flow of changes in an ongoing cycle of creative expression and knowledge building.

*We know nothing about a body (a person, a paintbrush, a pencil, a tube of paint, a kitchen) until we know what it can do, in other words what its affects are, how they can or cannot enter into composition with other affects, with the affects of another body.*

–Gilles Deleuze and Felix Guattari[9]

# listen

The cup was a potent protagonist of learning and becoming, not only for the children, but for us as well. Through listening, observing, documenting, dialoguing, questioning, thinking, and actively participating in events, we came to a new understanding of the vital role materials, objects, and artefacts play in creative expression and the construction of knowledge.

By opening our minds, hearts, and bodies to an uncertain, fluid, and emergent process of learning and becoming we became sensitised to the connective spaces in-between people, places, and things. We came to view ourselves as "connectors" and the creators of conditions where relationships can flourish, not only between people, places, and things, but also between ideas, strategies, languages of expression, and ways of knowing the world.

*When we broaden our capacity to listen
beyond human interaction we can
'hear' and observe other organisms,
objects and things around us 'speak.'
We become alert to their agency in
mutual processes of transformation
and learning.*

–Hillevi Lenz Taguchi[10]

# provoke

The cup as a vessel of potential and possibility goes on at Kids' Domain, and now hopefully, out there with you. As you live and learn in relationship with children we encourage you to listen carefully for the beckoning call of "things" for who knows where they may lead you.

We leave you with some questions that we hope provoke you to consider new pathways of joyful discovery in relationship with vibrant materials and things.

*What connections can you make between this story and your own work?*

*What new thoughts, ideas, and questions are inspired by this story?*

*What will you be listening for as you engage actively in collective inquiry?*

*How can you respond to what is happening in the "here and now" that opens up possibilities for creative expression and thought?*

*What new worlds might you bring forth in entangled relationship with others?*

# notes

1.  Ministry of Education, *Te Whāriki: He Whāriki Mātauranga mō ngā Mokopuna Aotearoa: Early Childhood Education* (Wellington: Learning Media, 1996), 9.

2.  Lella Gandini and Judith Allen Kaminsky, "Remida, the Creative Recycling Centre in Reggio Emilia: An Interview with Elena Giacopini, Graziella Brighenti, Arturo Bertoldi, and Alba Ferrari," *Innovations in Early Education* 12, no. 3 (2005), 1-13.

3.  Reggio Children, *Dialogue with Places* (Municipality of Reggio Emilia, Italy: Reggio Children, 2008), 44.

4.  Paola Cagliari, Marina Castagnetti, Claudia Giudici, Carlina Rinaldi, Vea Vecchi, and Peter Moss, eds. *Loris Malaguzzi and the Schools of Reggio Emilia: A Selection of His Writings and Speeches,1945-1993* (Oxon: Routledge, 2016), 349.

5.  Jane Bennett, *Vibrant Matter: A Political Ecology of Things* (Durham: Duke University Press, 2010), 6.

6.  Ann Pelo, *The Language of Art: Inquiry-based Studio Practices in Early Childhood Settings* (St. Paul: Redleaf Press, 2007).

7.  Jane Bennett, *Vibrant Matter: A Political Ecology of Things* (Durham: Duke University Press, 2010), 6.

8.  Ibid., viii.

9.  Gilles Deleuze and Felix Guattari, *A Thousand Plateaus: Capitalism and Schizophrenia*, trans. B. Massumi (Minneapolis: University of Minnesota Press, 1987), 257.

10. Hillevi Lenz Taguchi, *Going Beyond the Theory/Practice Divide in Early Childhood Education: Introducing an Intra-Active Pedagogy* (London: Routledge, 2010).

## From Reading to Thinking: A Protocol for Reflection and Learning

"The cup crept softly into our lives, an unexpected visitor," write Bridgette and Angela as their book begins. "At first we didn't think much of it, and then slowly, over time, it drew us deeper and deeper into encounter, continually challenging and provoking us to look and think differently" (p. 12).

Just so, we can allow ourselves to be drawn deeper and deeper into encounter with Bridgette and Angela's story, challenged by it to think differently. Inside the story of the cups is another story, a story about teaching—the story of "how it is possible to set aside predetermined outcomes to move *with* others in an emergent flow of events that is uncertain, and open to invention and creativity of thought" (p. 13).

The story of how cups lured children, their families, and educators into pursuing relationships with materials, testing their theories and representing their ideas, is compelling. The bold images of the children's cup constructions pulse with energy. You might be tempted to rush out to purchase a case of colorful cups, hoping to replicate the investigation of cups in your classroom. But that's not why Bridgette and Angela offer this story.

In their preface, they declare their intention to make their thinking, questioning, and decision-making visible, and they "invite you to think and question along with us." And they close their story with questions to provoke your thinking about your work, and how you understand collaborative inquiry and improvisational teaching. Alongside Bridgette and Angela's reflection questions, we offer a study protocol for you to use. This protocol is based on the Thinking Lens described in our book, *From Teaching to Thinking: A Pedagogy for Reimagining Our Work.* A protocol like the Thinking Lens is a tool for self-reflection and careful study; it provides a structure for conversations, and transforms "just talking" into pedagogical discussion. The Thinking Lens builds on the core principle of constructivism that people construct their understandings through experience and reflection—in this case, through reading the story of *Cup* and reflecting on how it relates to your current teaching practices.

Consider these protocol questions on your own, perhaps in writing, and then in conversation with colleagues and pedagogical companions.

### Know yourself. Open your heart to this moment.
What touched you about this story?

How were your values reflected or challenged by aspects of this story?

Did you have any "aha" moments as you read? About possibilities for children's play and learning? About possibilities for your teaching?

---

### Take the children's points of view.
What are the children trying to figure out in their work with cups?

What understandings, misunderstandings, and experiences are the children drawing on?

How are the children building on each other's ideas, perspectives, and contributions?

---

### Examine the environment.
How did the educators' understandings of the role of materials and the environment evolve during the exploration of cups?

How would you describe the social-emotional environment of this classroom?

---

**Collaborate with others to expand perspectives.**
What learning theories are you curious about after reading this story?

As you discuss this story with others, how are your perspectives or ideas challenged?

_____

**Reflect and take action.**
Building on your reflections, write a statement that describes the learning that you will carry with you from *Cup*.

What will you do differently in your work because of reading this book?

_____

Reading a book is an investment of time and attention. To make the most of that investment, revisit sections of the book that engaged or confused you. Find study companions to help you reflect on the story of *Cup*. Commit yourself to transforming your reading from a passive experience of listening to a good story to active engagement with thinking and questioning. Reading a book in this way becomes professional development.

As you carry *Cup* into your teaching practice, may you find energizing opportunities to embody the verbs at the heart of the book: *construct, transform, collaborate, imagine, listen, shift, investigate, reflect, theorize, provoke, connect.*

**—Ann Pelo** and **Margie Carter**
   Editors of the *Reimagining Our Work* (ROW) Collection
   Authors of *From Teaching to Thinking: A Pedagogy for Reimagining Our Work*

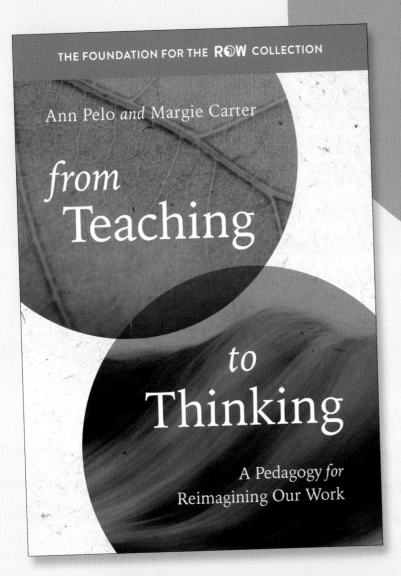